Reflections Of A Goddess
Written By: Sheri Hannibal

Table Of Contents

This Book is:
Dedicated to the late Mary Carter Hannibal
The best grandmother ever
I love you always!
And to my two beautiful children …
Skye and Journey, I do it for you!

Our Mary

Our Mary who art in heaven that will be her name
Since you left the earth this family hasn't been the same
We forgot about can salmon, collard greens, sausages, okra, tomato, and rice
We don't even remember sweet potato bread, coconut custard pie, sit up gossiping late night
We can't even acknowledge   how the food from your soul held us together
These days we on our own path don't got time for each other
Every Sunday, holiday, even during the week you brought life
Your where the best grandmother, your bond with each one of us was tight
Oldest granddaughter, they called me on the phone that's how I had to hear
I'm so sorry I wasn't there
I heard our GOD call for you mid-day, it was in your sleep that's how he took you away
We see it as a sad death, but in reality, he took you gentle, easy, slow, show's your so blessed
He didn't want you to hurt
O!!! But when they sat your coffin in that hole and covered it with dirt
All your energy, to us it came
We were the one left in pain
Our Mary who art in heaven that will be her name

Intellectual Girl

She was taught by the best educators to be an intellectual
When she spoke, she gave the room
A feel of the sun on a summer day
Modest in every way
Seen scholarly not sexually
Her words would downpour in your head
Like hot tar hitting the pavement
She explains herself as if she was an angel
Perch on a cloud with a halo
She was so well-spoken that she could
describe the texture on a maple
And the sound that water makes when it splashes
you wish you were there
She would talk about victory
so well that you crumble in your seat
And begged her for more
There was no need for them to tell her
that she was an intellectual
She detected herself,
She was taught by the best educators to be an intellectual

RAIN FOREST

Deep in the rainforest, your way was lost, you got distracted by the pink mushrooms, blue lakes, and jack frost,
Go ahead try, lay it on thick to the fruits in this garden, here glorify words won't earn you a pardon

Hard work, long haul, tough grind, will get the ship in the harbor
In the rainforest, you got to put in work to see the fruits of your labor

Deep In the rain forest if you try the milk you must buy the cow, sipping and walking away is not allowed

Over the hill under the bridge pass the cake with the white icing
Pine rope to the left, apple on your right, No eating the pineapple unless your splicing
Be careful no staring, no enticing
Tie the cherries in a knot use the white grapes for ricing

If you get acquainted share jokes, giggle, laugh
Don't hesitate to take the white path

You reach in your pocket realize you don't have a dime
You don't want to work or pay for it, but you still want a sip of cherry wine

Only the strong, the proud, and few
Are allowed to dine

Down the street passed the gate, you speed up you realize you're late

The thought of losing was hard to chew
But she's gone now all cause you didn't wanna say I DO...

IM DONE !!!

You've hurt me to the core, so much so I don't want you anymore..
.you've stabbed my heart 8 times if I give you a 9th I'm done...
It's best if I take off, and run...
I need to take cover from your storm cause the lies don't drizzle they pour.....
You give as much respect as a priest gives the devil,
you comprised with me like a pill on an empty stomach,
 you're, not the solution you're the problem,
you bring the issues you don't solve them
 I trust you like a thief if in the night,
a mosquito ready to suck blood and bite…
 Like a dog you mark your territory and walk away not caring you shited on someone's lawn,
 they have to clean it up today, they have to, not you..
.you made the mess but left it for someone else to endure...
You deserve less not more…...
 You're, not the victim, you're the offender …
you can't end it, cause you started it...
You can't be used because you are the user,
 you can't be hurt cause you're the abuser...
I will not allow you to control me anymore, pack your bags, get out, move in with that whore...
Hurry up, grab your things, say goodby to the home-cooked meals, your kids, and clean house..
Let me show you to the door...
I won't invest another dime of my precious time in you… ..
straight down the street to the left, you've been over there a million timed I'm sure you know the rest...
I'm strongest enough to catch every stone you threw I'm wise enough to get rid of you...

I Am Woman

I am who I am,
 I'm a product of my environment who strives to be better.
 I am a broken black woman struggling to beat the odds.
 I am a very important women because I control the future and destiny of my offspring
 I am a gift from God to the black man
 I am a demanding women who wants respect by any means necessary
 I am a cautious women searching for understanding
 I am my daughter chastity keeper
 I am my son example of loving a black women
 I am a stereo types who wants to beat the odds
 I am a child of a higher power
 I am a lover not a fighter
 I am the queen of my castle
 I am the keeper of my domain
 I am the earth rotating around the sun
 I am a understanding but unstable, listening, women
 I am a finger pointer with direction
 I am a dreamer
 I am far away places, exotic lands, blue water
 I am hardcore on the inside only to guard my heart
 I am a woman of many layers
 I am broken hearted, misunderstood,
 i am a breath of fresh air in an open room,
 I am a overcomer,
 I pray every sec to live another day,
 I am the chair in the room no one wants to sit on,
 I am the writing on the wall people forget to read ,
 I am who I am, that's all I will ever be I'm proud of me
 I am who I am that's all can be
 the mistakes I made I'm not upset about them so why should you be
 I am who I am that's all I could be
 I can't be who you want me to be
 I have to deal with my problems because they happen to me
 I'm not upset about it so why should you be
 I am who I am that's all I can be

Loyalty

The problem with loyalty is everyone has their own opinion...
Men of the law catch you in a compromising position
Your chill buddy taken to a room for simple questioning
Words from your so call homeboy lips will decide, your independence or incarceration
You sit in the other blocked room in deep concentration, trying to figure out how you got in this position
Your whole life flashes before your eyes
your life held in the hands of another man truth or lies

problem with loyalty everybody got their own opinion
In your mind, you start questioning
is his loyalty to you or the detective doing the session
His Loyalty to the rules of the streets or walking by giving up a confession
You realize that's my main man he'll never punk out
Wipe that sweat, chill out!

robbing, stick ups, killings, you and dude got each other back straight chillin
Clubbing, women, shopping, drug dealing
You saw 1 you saw the other
Y'all did it all together
Even when you ate, you made sure ya man's had a plate

Two men walk in the door suited from head to toe
They tell to stand, turn, put your hands behind you back its time to go
He told us you had the 45 you made the pop
You like naw, dude made the final shot
Too late now he free
He walks, goes home to his family

Word on the street dude don't know your name
That whole friendship thing you thought y'all had, it was a game
You writing home, dude lame

Lesson learned ,he's not in reality
He picks his freedom 1st
That's his opinion of loyalty

Delusional

We belong together - You know this
From the touch of your hand to your smooth, kiss
When I look into my future, I see you there
I cannot imagine you anywhere but here
I know the more bruises you give
Just mean you care
But when i say i'm leaving, you start crying
Are those crocodile tears ?
I really do have these feelings -I really care
That black eye is nothing i can't bear
A couple of ice cubes it will clear
I like the way you touch me; the way you makes me feel
When I say I love you, there's No need to slap me baby I'm not lying I really am keeping it real
No worries bae, that chair didn't hit me
I used my arm as a shield
Life is to short for us to be apart
I'm still mesmerize, by when you told me that I held the key to your heart
When I lay next to you, and here you say " I love you girl"
That makes me feel 100% good I feel like
I could conquer the world
When you come in at 4 am just wake me
Don't worry about yesterday
The doctor said that burn was only 3rd degree
I love you honey
I feel like we are going to be together forever and a day
I found someone to patch that hole in the wall
And since im super tall
The glass you threw hit my shoulder
My face it missed
Bae, you're right ! My friends are jealous our love exist
They think you meant to break my wrist
 I know that isn't true
Cause' you love me and I love you
I apologize for screaming when you pulled my hair
Im ok Just a little of my scalp has teared
It's been 3 days honey, come back to me
Your sadly missed
We belong together - you know this
From the touch of your hand to your smooth, kiss

Understanding of Life

We all shed tears
We all have our crosses to bear
We all have done wrong
We all fall short
We all lose strength

> When simple things make you smile
> It makes the love worthwhile
> The joy of having more for less
> Makes living life feel bless

We all endure pain
We all lost a loved one too soon
We all are scorn
We all had a broken heart a time or two
We all needed to be carried by our savior;
  At some point in life

> When simple things make you smile
> It makes the love worthwhile
> The joy of having more for less
> Makes living life feel bless

The struggle is real
The reward is so much better
Be strong, stay focus, let your Savior take the wheel
Dreams meet reality through hard work
Practice what you preach
Share what you know
Give life a chance
From it, you will grow

> When simple things make you smile
> It makes the love worthwhile
> The joy of having more for less
> Makes living life feel bless

Coffee spot...

I traveled this road daily
On a Monday dressed in Sunday best
Looking like a lady, out to impress
Gather at a coffee spot
Reminisce with other retires
Grandchildren, nowadays, hot topics
One cream, two sugars, I sip
Out the windows I glance
Beautiful flowers and sunsets remind me of Romance
I want to get closer to be amazed by the charm
One push of the door off goes the alarm
People in uniforms rush to pull me back
"Mrs.Libby it's time for your nap"
I pray I paid my debt to society
Believe I gave it all I got
All I remember today is my coffee spot
Long for them to see my strength even when I'm weak
I wish they know even though I can't remember I still can teach
I dream my family knows I still love visits, car rides, hugs, and to shop
But today all I can remember is this coffee spot
Ask to phone the love of my life
MRS. LIBBY 3yrs ago your husband was token by Jesus Christ
"News to me, I wasn't told, call a cop" !
"Mrs.Libby let's take a walk back to your coffee spot"
Steaming hot;
One cream, two sugars, I sip,
Cause, today all I remember is my coffee spot

Friends to foes

Aquiences sharing thoughts
Associate connecting in mind
and soul
Companions hanging together
Non-lovers having feelings for each other
touching in a sociable way
Hanging together on a friendly day
Ending with a sexual bliss ,
Saying goodbye with a forehead kiss
No commitment, just benefits
late night moan,
holding down that friend zone
Putting each other in unfamiliar position
Arguments began to flare
One of you don't care
One of you in your feeling and want the others heart
But you agreed just friends from the start
No longer friends-
How is this?

Materialized

Before all else I saw you in a dream
Came on like a movie
It was a romance scene
At first sight it was blurry
It felt like a page from a love story
With my own two eyes a soul was seen
Floated across the room in ghostly form
What was once two became one human being
In my presence in front of my own eyes
Your soul materialized
It floated towards me with ease
Like it needed my expertise
The Aura of the soul hover over me
As if it was ready to risk it all for love
Even though there's no guarantees
I can't explain or understand
But I witnessed
The soul of one woman and one man
With the snap of a finger from Jesus
 God's only forsaken son
Become materialized in to one

Wintummer

Summer and Winter the Therapist will see you now....

I hope seeing this doctor helps us adjust

 Summer a lot people need help getting along, it's okay to see a Therapist

They tried to say last year I was a bummer

I don't care about your problems
Summer
 I have my issues too .....
Hiking, camping, long walks slow down with me, but picks back up when they get to you

You bring families back together
You have Christmas time and comfort food for dinner

I know ..... I know .....
everyone likes cozying by the fireplace, watching movies, sipping hot chocolate just because I'm Winter

Last year I did some stuff you wouldn't believe

So who cares, I made it snow on Christmas Eve

You also get the pleasure of bringing in the New Year

Summer, please stop with the crocodile tears

I had the beaches pack, with my triple digits over a 100 degrees

Netflix owes me a check for the whole stay in and chill

due to overheating people use too much air, I helped increase those energy bills

Really !!! I thought it would drop
Cause of the cookouts, traveling, and hanging at the ice cream shops

They complain non-stop....
What do they want ?

With you it is too cold ...
With me it's too hot....

Summer I'm tired of hearing you whimper

I heard people started getting really sick back in December

Look summer they shut the world down in March ....
Don't you remember ?

Don't throw that on me , it was spring

Let's get to the point
Are you responsible for this covid 19 thing

Winter, blaming a world pandemic on me isn't okay

Rather you started it or not
Get ready, cause I think it's here to stay

He walks in blackness

Glistening crown
Full smile, showing gladness
Dripping in Royalty
He walks in blackness
Making ancestor proud
Gliding like a brush across a canvas
Draped in purple and gold
With his head held high
He walks in blackness
Men of the law trying to break him down with all their tactics
Always gets look over
Sometimes Mistreated
Pushed hard to win
Most times gets defeated
Cause '
He walks in blackness
On the prowl for a natural queen
Never intrigued by a perm or weave
Mesmerized by realness
Blinded by actresses
He'll commit to any shade
Appreciates all sizes
A king needs his queen
To support him as
He walks in blackness

Husband to be

Your spirit
The drive
So motivated
It's sexy
A turn on
It's so Exhilarating
A man with a hustle
A plan
And gives a damn
A heart like gold
Deep like Neo-Soul
A muse for my creative side
Maybe a husband ?
Well I asked...
At least I tried !
Candy for my conscience
Easy on the eye
So much honesty
Never a lie
In black man I trust
Not white currency
Claim your queen
Challenge me daily
Earn your crown
I'll be forever grateful
And never will let you down

I said No !!!!

What part of No isn't understood
The N or the O
When I say leave
Turn around and go
I said No !!
I'm glad we were once friends
Im sure I enjoyed you a time or two
But now I have other things going on
And I said No !!!
I'm not playing hard to get
New dude keeps me giddy and wet
Yeah !!! he took your place
With ease,style and grace
Sorry if your still alone
Bads times are temporary
 I pray you find someone of your own
I can't help you I have a beau
Stop trying over here
I said No !!!
You feel the love in the air !!!
Can you see the glow ?
Signs I've move on
So once again
I said No !!!!
Please listen and let go
As a woman I have the right to choose
And to you I'm saying no
Stop inboxing, texting, calling, or emailing
 Not looking for multiple men
I'm not a hoe
I SAID NO !!!!!!!

Reflections Of A Goddess

From the light I see my Reflection
Sweet , tan, like caramel corn
Like the pot, always used and needed
 Burnt and scorned;
 breath of life fogs up the image
Through the smudge
I see the sin
Here lies me
 A shiny reflection of what's within
Dark as a pitted hole
Clear as day
Glistening like a diamond
Covered in gold
But only two foot steps,
none are my own
I never walked alone
Seems like I was carried half the way
God is real ,He heard me pray
Even when I sinned
Had nothing but evil with-in
I was escorted to the end
forgiving without judgement of my sin
giving another chance to do it again
This time I'll walk with grace
My head held high
Focus on becoming a woman who is modest
So next time in my reflection
I'll see a Goddess ......

Follow me @

Youtube   Reflections OF A Goddess
Gmail   Reflectionsofablackgoddess@gmail.com
Instagram   reflections_of_a_goddess

About The Author

Sheri Hannibal was born in Paterson, N.J. ,but raised in Paterson and Sumter, S.C.

She was born the oldest child of one brother.

She has been writing since the age of 12, she published her first poem to poetry.com.

She now lives in Sumter, S.C., and is tall for no reason. No, she doesn't play basketball or volleyball, she writes great poetry.

About The Book

Reflections Of A Goddess was created with you in mind. Whether you're trying to relax, read something inspirational, or need a good read for a quiet moment this book is exactly what the doctor ordered. These inspirational poems deliver a big zest of flavors to warm your soul.

Never looking back
Only looking forward to better days
Sheri T Hannibal

The beginning , Never the end
Sheri T Hannibal

By:

Sheri T Hannibal
Volume 1

The End

Made in the USA
Columbia, SC
28 October 2022

70146068R00015